Michael Timpson

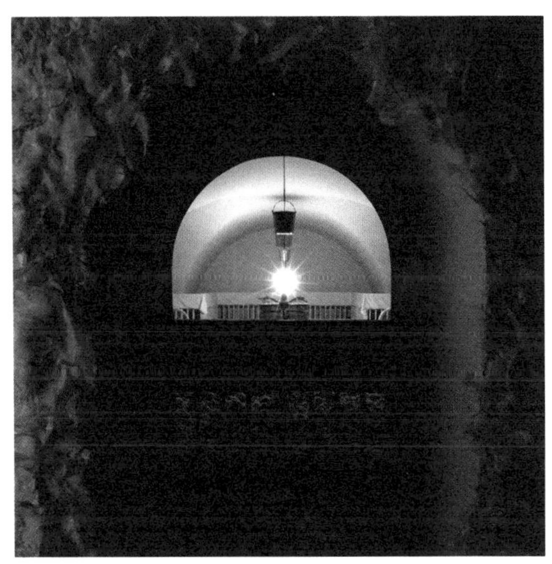

Huston Paschal

November 2, 1991–February 2, 1992

North Carolina Museum of Art
Raleigh, North Carolina

Acknowledgments

An installation makes extraordinary demands on a museum. For the resilience and cooperation of the entire North Carolina Museum of Art staff, I am grateful. To Tom Lopez, Design Production Head, a special thanks is due. The Museum relies on his resourcefulness in getting any show mounted, and never more so than in this case. In addition, two unstinting participants in this enterprise, Martin Breeson, the artist's assistant and chief wrapper, and carpenter and artist Graham Auman, are to be commended. Another valuable member of the team was builder Fairley Monroe. David B. Greene, Coordinator of the Art Studies Program at North Carolina State University, Raleigh, also enthusiastically entered into the spirit of the undertaking. His endorsement led to critical hands-on assistance from a bevy of university students, chief among whom were David Beck and Joseph Fulghum. The Triangle area and beyond responded in a heartening way to various outlandish requests. Materials and services were provided by Agri Supply Company, Brothers Pizza Restaurants, Bull City Bicycles, Camps Sea Gull and Seafarer, Carolinas Cotton Growers Association, Duke Medical Center, Jim Sparr Drywall, Rex Hospital, and Servitex, Inc.

Working with Michael Timpson has been a treat, and I am happy to acknowledge my debt to him. His installation, *"But the Ball Is Lost and the Mallet Slipped,"* is a thrilling (if disobedient) way to inaugurate the Museum's new exhibition space.

H.P.

Incorrigibly Plural

A Michael Timpson installation can confound. Its elements, familiar and organized according to an obvious, rational plan, are conjoined with puzzling consequences. Viewers immediately recognize the sheets and towels, the bread and turkey feathers, the open books and sealed body bags. As readily, the inherent contradictions emerge. An observer discovers confrontations between the punctilious and the subversive, the solemn and the irreverent, the sacred and the profane. Timpson, an adept equivocator, entangles substance and speculation in his dramatic, walk-through installations. With the flair of a ringmaster, he lures viewers in. Drawing on his childhood in rural Ireland and his Catholic background, the artist mounts a morality play, modern in its inconclusiveness.

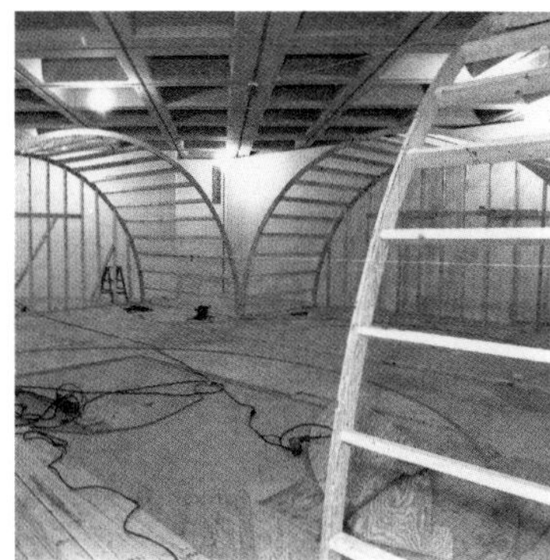

In ten years of constructing these perplexing environments with their built-in humor, Timpson has codified a formal and conceptual vocabulary. On a perfectly plotted grid, the space is punctuated by objects called to order in unyielding symmetry. (Which can produce some curious cohabitants: A quartet of push brooms supervises four simmering eggs. Heads of cabbage bracket lines of laundry. Granite boulders escort aluminum basins down a boardwalk.) A sense of unimpeachable placement prevails. Color is reined in as well; whiteness preponderates.

The imposition of order, the repetition of forms, and the clarion chromaticism have a certain predictability about them. Reading about previous pieces—documentation of which is, of course, all that remains—one comes to know what to expect. Serried ranks of army cots in one installation are followed by clean columns of garbage cans in another and parallel rows of feed sacks in a third. The rectangle-within-a-rectangle is used as a way of organizing space in several pieces. The rhythm of arrangement—paired boulders resting on paired bleachers—animating one installation is found elsewhere, in books and pillows ranked three by three, and spades and wheelbarrows grouped four by four. And always, a starched whiteness predominates, sometimes bordered in black, perhaps pricked by crimson.

To discuss this work from the floor plan up does justice to the spruce, on-the-surface orderliness, but it fails to take into account the overt theatricality. Characterized by the finiteness of a stage set, a Timpson "blueprint" also makes room for the interaction of entrenched doubts and unplumbed mysteries. This artist shares sense and sensibility with Samuel Beckett. Timpson's formal means are as terse as Beckett's scripts, and his spare, spectral lighting locates viewers on the twilight edge of certainty where the late Irish playwright's audiences find themselves.

Such an atmosphere releases the abstractions clambering among the specified. To furnish his lean architecture, Timpson amasses the mundane—with a rigged result: His box-like constructions abound with metaphorical associations and assertive ambiguities. Incorporating some found objects, he mostly relies on commodities sought out and purchased for both their in-stock ordinariness and their mint condition. They are to bring no history with them; it is the artist who enlarges upon their iconography. These utilitarian items now function not so much as stage props, but as protagonists.

Tools and equipment cloistered in the chapel-like retreat *"Just Knock Three Times and Whisper Low"* (see p. 13) pay homage to the common laborer. Bearing witness to the discipline such an occupation demands, spades and wheelbarrows are partnered with a martial crispness. Reverence for the working man is a recurring motif in Timpson's work. It is joined by a sympathetic theme, one that examines the uneasy coexistence of authority and individuality. The objects that Timpson brings together adumbrate this rivalry; they remain discrete units yet are made to conform to rules of a communal order. A human being lives with a similar dichotomy; he must balance

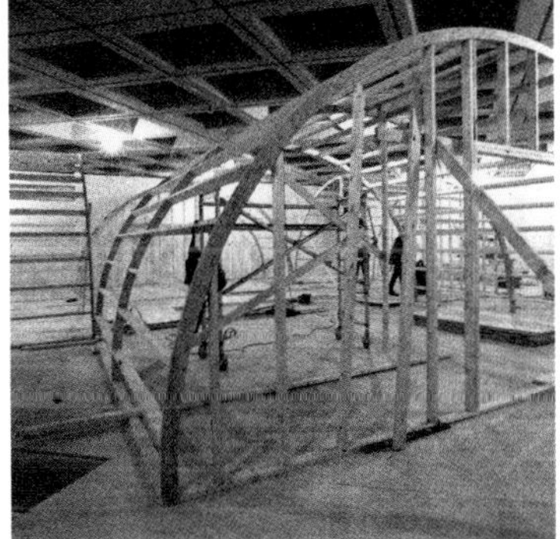

the urge to maintain a sense of personal identity with the need to believe in something bigger than himself.

Prepotent and omnipresent, the Church, specifically the Roman Catholic church under whose aegis Timpson grew up and went to school, makes a convenient subject for exploring this issue. Evocations of church ritual and regalia (references to the sacraments, paraphrases of altars and prie-dieus, and allusions to priests and prayer) are rife in Timpson's work. The artist uses them to address the dualities knotted in the overarching power of the Church—its allure as refuge, its threat to the unorthodox. His piece for the North Carolina Museum

of Art, *"But the Ball Is Lost and the Mallet Slipped,"* is an ambitious structure, cruciform in shape, which exerts dominion over its 3,000-square-foot gallery. The arms of Timpson's explicitly Latin cross are actually covered corridors large enough to accommodate human traffic, an ingenious rendering of the all-protective embrace of the Church. (A typical Timpson touch—instead of being jewel-encrusted, this cross is covered with turkey feathers.)

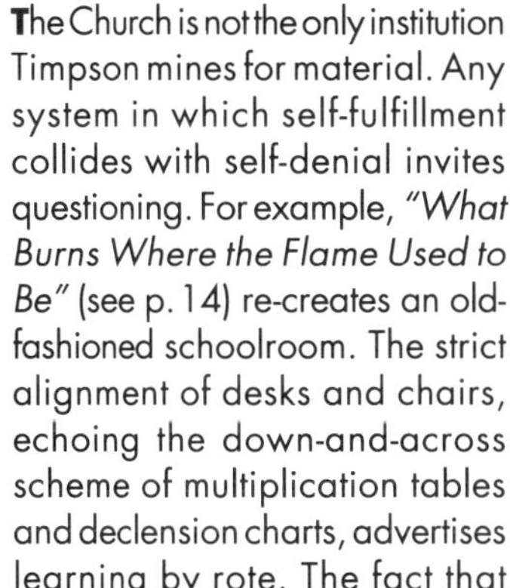

The Church is not the only institution Timpson mines for material. Any system in which self-fulfillment collides with self-denial invites questioning. For example, *"What Burns Where the Flame Used to Be"* (see p. 14) re-creates an old-fashioned schoolroom. The strict alignment of desks and chairs, echoing the down-and-across scheme of multiplication tables and declension charts, advertises learning by rote. The fact that each chair is out of scale—putting the student in an awkward position at his desk and undermining his study—shapes the statement into criticism of an impersonal methodology with misplaced priorities. The "teacher" presiding is a television, turned on but tuned to grainy, buzzing nothingness. What conclusions are to be drawn? That a machine is no replacement for the human touch? That pedagogical techniques are out of focus? Maybe the blank screen stands for the unseen but ominous presence of an Orwellian Big Brother. There is another possibility: the static may be in the heads of the pupils, whose presence is only implied. Not yet brainwashed, they may just be lost in thought.

Ambiguity crowds the confident design. Books, for instance, which appear frequently in Timpson's installations, are freighted with multiple inferences. The volumes, always big and always open, stand for the Bible or, more generally, for knowledge. The same object thus ironically represents the laid-down law of the Church and the opening up of a mind. But the way in which the books are invariably presented—as compromised objects of devotion—checks a zealot's trust in Bible *or* bible, proposing instead a healthy, if heretical, skepticism.

Timpson ransoms tradition from tired thinking—and rescues each installation's fastidious regularity from stasis. Plundering an arsenal of sensory weaponry, he brings the prim enclave to life by injecting sound, activity, even smells. The "pick, pack, pock, puck" (to appropriate James Joyce's onomatopoeia) of water dripping into a tin bucket registers a pulse. In other works, the pace is comically accelerated by the agitated ticking of clocks, their syncopated sound heard by some as the duple rhythm of a heartbeat and by others as the gripping countdown of an explosive. Viewer involvement adds its own movement and generates its own noise; footfalls orchestrate the clatter of boardwalks, the crunch of gravel paths. In an outdoor installation (see p. 16), bed sheets flap in the breeze, providing both snap and motion. Indoors, boxer shorts sway gently in the air circulating through a museum gallery (see p. 17). The olfactory sense is not shortchanged. In fact, it may be accosted by the salient aromas of moist topsoil, freshly sawn lumber, rotting potatoes, moldy Wonder Bread, or oozing lake sludge.

That many of the surfaces in these installations are wrapped in fabric also mollifies the sharp-edged rectilinearity of the governing grid. Bicycles, shovels, buckets—all are apt to be draped or swathed. This rite elevates the commonplace to the ceremonial, the cloth's bleached whiteness enveloping these new relics in an aura of purity. Church ritual has a grace and glamour that appeal and reassure. Timpson succeeds in transferring these qualities to his secular instruments of faith, making them available to believers and nonbelievers alike.

The masking, which sometimes extends to the human figure (in the flesh and in effigy), operates on other levels. Typically, the ramifications double back on themselves. Blindfolding, a traditional emblem of spiritual shortsightedness, in Timpson's hands also intimates the intangible that man must accept without proof. Further, the swaddling offsets the suggestion of danger, or at least discomfort, that is sometimes present. The pristine is sullied by noisome smells, disrupted by jangling alarms. Courtly decorum is violated by pinched entrances and obstructed walkways. Below-normal temperatures and above-normal humidity disconcert. Sheathed, shrouded, and padded surfaces (the installations often are studded with pillows, too) cushion viewers, at least figuratively. For every effect, there is a countereffect.

The straightforward ground plan belies the labyrinth of meaning it supports—or conceals, with Timpson's mixed signals eliciting some farfetched (and maybe not so farfetched) extrapolating. Numerologists discern significance in the specific numbers—and

Timpson is content to let them, though to him it is the symmetry that matters. Exegetes detect connotations in the choice of text and where it falls open, but it is size and typography that lie behind book and page selection. (The fact that in one of his installations the *Congressional Record* rests on a toilet, suggestive of a Bible on a prie-dieu, is explained not by politics but by circumstance. The artist's request to a bookstore for volumes of a precise size turned up only one title— the *Record*.) Timpson relishes the multiplicity of interpretations, dismissing none out of hand. About his work the artist has said, "What people bring to it is its meaning."

A key to the conundrum cannot be fashioned from the titles. Some (like *"What Burns Where the Flame Used to Be"*) are refrains from nineteenth-century Irish street ballads, and some are lines of verse chosen at random from anthologies of English and Irish poetry. Others adopt colloquial expressions favored by family and friends or associated with episodes in Timpson's boyhood. The lyric on which a William Butler Yeats poem is based and the excerpts from Percy Bysshe Shelley and Pádraic Pearse* may be as identifiable as the objects assembled for the installations. But beyond that, their relationship to the work itself is enigmatic. As for the sayings and punch lines, one needs help only the artist can give in understanding

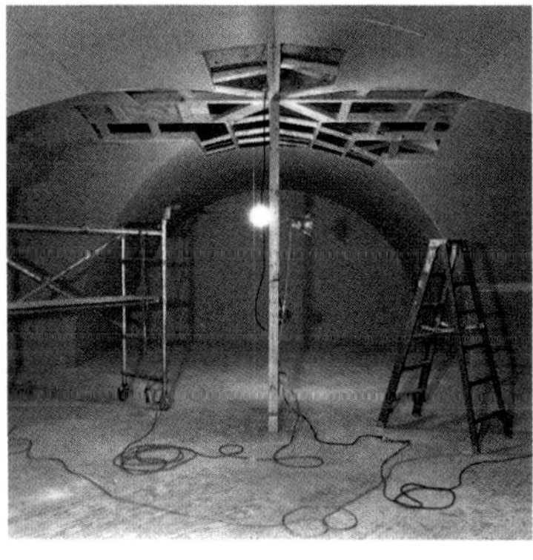

"be the boys," "bearing the rabbit," and "the Mickey ruz." His explanations, colorful and convoluted, establish the origin of the phrases but not their tie-in to the installations.

Two examples demonstrate how the titles resist diagnosis. *"Just Knock Three Times and Whisper Low"* is the name given the contemplative setting with wheelbarrows and spades as its magnetic centerpiece; it comes from *The Pajama Game.* The exact source is "Hernando's Hideaway," a song which the three Timpson brothers used to sing in bed, after lights-out. For Timpson to disclose this information is not to give away secrets. The riddle revolving around Hollywood musical, sibling shenanigans, and sincere tribute to the world's wage earners remains. Another work, showcasing a spirited parade of sheets across a meadow, is called *"He Will Not Come and Still I Wait,"* its name chosen—Timpson avers—by his aleatory system. However, learning that this piece was done soon after his father's death makes one suspect some deliberateness in the selection of its poignantly elegiac title. The additional discovery that Timpson nudges chance by intentionally misquoting citations corners his audience in confusion. About his work in general, the artist flatly states, "The title has no connection to the piece." Warily, one takes him at his word.

---

*Another Irishman from whom Timpson has borrowed is Louis MacNiece, whose poem "Soap Suds" is the source for the title of the artist's North Carolina Museum of Art installation. (The title of this essay, by the way, also comes from a MacNiece poem, "Snow.")

Timpson comes rightly by his way with words. He grew up listening to the fabulous talk of an eccentric grandmother—who immersed him in the darkly romantic lore of pre-Celtic Ireland—and acceded to a rich literary inheritance. Equally fascinated by the story recorded in the island's megalithic remains, this is an artist influenced more by words than by art. Recollecting and reconstructing his childhood and his country's legends and myths, Timpson invests his work with his autobiography. His meaning is expressed in "the language of memory," to borrow a phrase from *A Portrait of the Artist as a Young Man,* a book by an Irishman who also drew on the bank of personal experience.

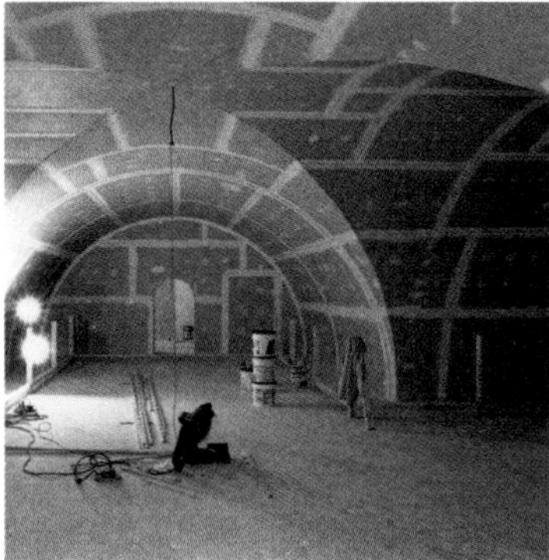

Anyone conversant with James Joyce's self-referential novel should feel at home in Timpson's installations. Evidence of congenial sensitivities builds, from similarities in minor details, to invocations of Shelley, to preoccupation with the same searching inquiries into the role of the Church and the nature of creativity. Reading *Portrait* and thinking of Timpson, one is struck by Joyce's emphatic use of the black, white, and red that color the installations. Repeatedly, the same smells Joyce's alter ego Stephen Dedalus encounters (for example, "the rainsodden earth gave forth its mortal odour") assail viewers, as do the sounds Dedalus hears. (When, for instance, Joyce/Dedalus describes "the ticking of a great clock. . . . and it seemed to this saint that the sound of the ticking was the ceaseless repetition of the words: ever, never; ever, never," it recalls the two-beat chorus of the timepieces in *"Bearing the Rabbit."*)

There is also the connection between Timpson's labyrinths and Stephen's last name.

More pointedly, the turns of phrase Dedalus uses in talking about art and religion could as well illustrate Timpson's work and thought. Dedalus dwells on words, struggling with them to define beauty, elaborating on "the rhythm of its structure" and the "esthetic stasis . . . at last dissolved." This nomenclature is applicable to the installations, too. When Dedalus perceives a priest's service in terms of "the thrill of . . . obedience," it makes one think of the discipline Timpson imposes with such highly charged results. The Church is a looming presence; as for Dedalus, so for Timpson, it mingles intimacy with alienation, inspiring feelings of awe and impotence. Dedalus's attraction to the priesthood—its "vague acts . . . pleased him by reason of their semblance of reality and of their distance from it"—offers insight into Timpson's constructs.

The subsequent conclusion of Joyce's novitiate manqué, that Catholicism is "an absurdity which is logical and coherent," better describes Timpson's art than his attitude toward the Church. (Though no longer a practicing Catholic, he is not anticlerical.) The artist lends the logic and coherence of his installations to a theater of the absurd. And his social commentary exploits (often to humorous effect) the fineness of the line between stage performance and church ritual. Timpson's jeux d'esprit—an ersatz liturgy parodying the celebration of the Mass, the visiting of the stations of the cross—

unfold in the calibrated sequence that drama and storytelling require. The visual "pace" established by the metrical arrangement is dignified; step by step, placement after placement is apprehended. With a storyteller's instinct, Timpson directs the viewer's progress along succinctly demarcated paths.

Control is a concept central to this work. *"Now Do You Know,"* important in the artist's development, was the first time he so thoroughly manipulated the environment (exposing people to chilling temperatures and ill lit, wobbly walkways). Since that piece, Timpson has subjected participants to increasing constraints; passive observation has been replaced by a more total, physical experience. The control factor is embodied in the installations by containers: Sacks and vats and buckets. Coffinlike repositories and body bags. Basins and saucepans, wheelbarrows and garbage cans. Even armchairs and beds can fairly be construed as belonging in this category, as can fences and balustrades. Furthermore, each installation is a self-contained entity.

Containers impose order. Timpson's mastery of paradox expands their role, making them into another double-sided metaphor, a message equal parts sentence and reprieve. Walls—that fix boundaries—enclose chambers that are the site of change. Bags of rice, universal symbol of fertility, occupy places of honor in one installation. Another is accentuated by sacks bulging with soft, moist earth—redolent of Irish bogs—from which signs of life spring forth. But Timpson turns the meaning in-

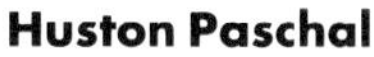

side out, creating a Möbius strip of ambivalence. *"It's a Far Cry"* (see p. 18), the same work in which the hope of regeneration is represented by rice, centers around a marriage bed, its promise splintered by the disquieting nails on which it rests.

As even-handed as dilemma, Timpson declines to take sides in the interplay between limitation and possibility. The artist's thinking has been much influenced by Ireland's prehistoric burial mounds; the graves' restrictive passageways define an interval between being in and being out—a transitional zone—that is key to the philosophy of this self-exile. Timpson perceives that in just such a tenuous slot does man reside, shuttling back and forth in a "ceaseless . . . ever, never" rhythm between the predetermined and the unknown. (These polarities are themselves malleable—seen by some as sanctuary and risk, by others as custody and license.) And it is just such a space, tenebrous and dense with interrogation and innuendo, that the artist realizes in his installations.

Huston Paschal
Associate Curator of Modern Art

"But the Ball Is Lost and the Mallet Slipped"

North Carolina Museum of Art, Raleigh

November 2, 1991–February 2, 1992

A short passageway requiring viewers to duck their heads and step onto a ramp led right and then left, opening into a 3,000-square-foot gallery. Inside on an elevated plywood floor, a vaulted structure, its footprint a Latin cross, dominated the space. It was positioned on the diagonal, with the longer arm of the cross extending toward the entrance. Spread over the floor around this cruciform construction was a thick layer of loose, unfolded pages of the local newspaper. At each of the four exterior corners made by the cross's intersecting arms, a single bulb hidden in a coffer above provided feeble light. The arms—tunnel vaults large enough to walk through—were made of plywood ribs, faced inside with gypsum board and outside with plywood, both

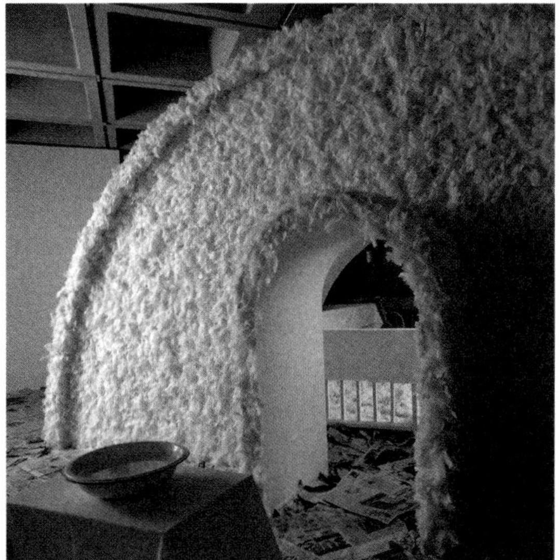

painted white. As the plywood was painted, a layer of white turkey feathers was "glued" to its wet surface. A wall sealed the end of each arm, and three of the walls (the long one and the two side arms) were inset, producing three-inch soffits. Placed in front of each of these three end walls was a small, high table, its legs wrapped in white fabric and its top draped with a white cloth; a white enameled basin filled with water sat on each table.

The wall of the long arm contained a small, arched entryway. Maneuvering around the table and stooping to pass through this opening, one found in each arm of the structure an old-fashioned bicycle, parked facing the center. Each bicycle was wrapped, from fender and spokes to handlebars, in white fabric. (Retired hospital bed sheets torn into narrow strips were used to do the wrapping throughout the installation.) The bicycles stood on a bed of ginned cotton. Suspended from a rope above each bicycle was a galvanized steel pail. In the center, under the point where the arms met in a groin vault, there was a circular farm trough of galvanized steel resting on a mound of institutional, stainless steel knives and forks.

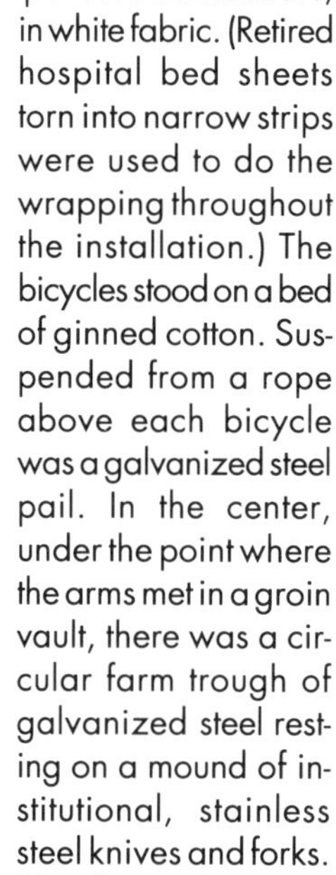

The trough, two feet high and four feet in diameter, was filled with molasses. Over it hung a bare, dim bulb, the only illumination for the chamber. A continuous walkway, its surface covered with newspapers, outlined the interior perimeter of the cross shape. It was bordered by a balustrade, the balusters wrapped in white and the railing draped with starched sheeting. The narrow path crowded visitors against the curved walls.

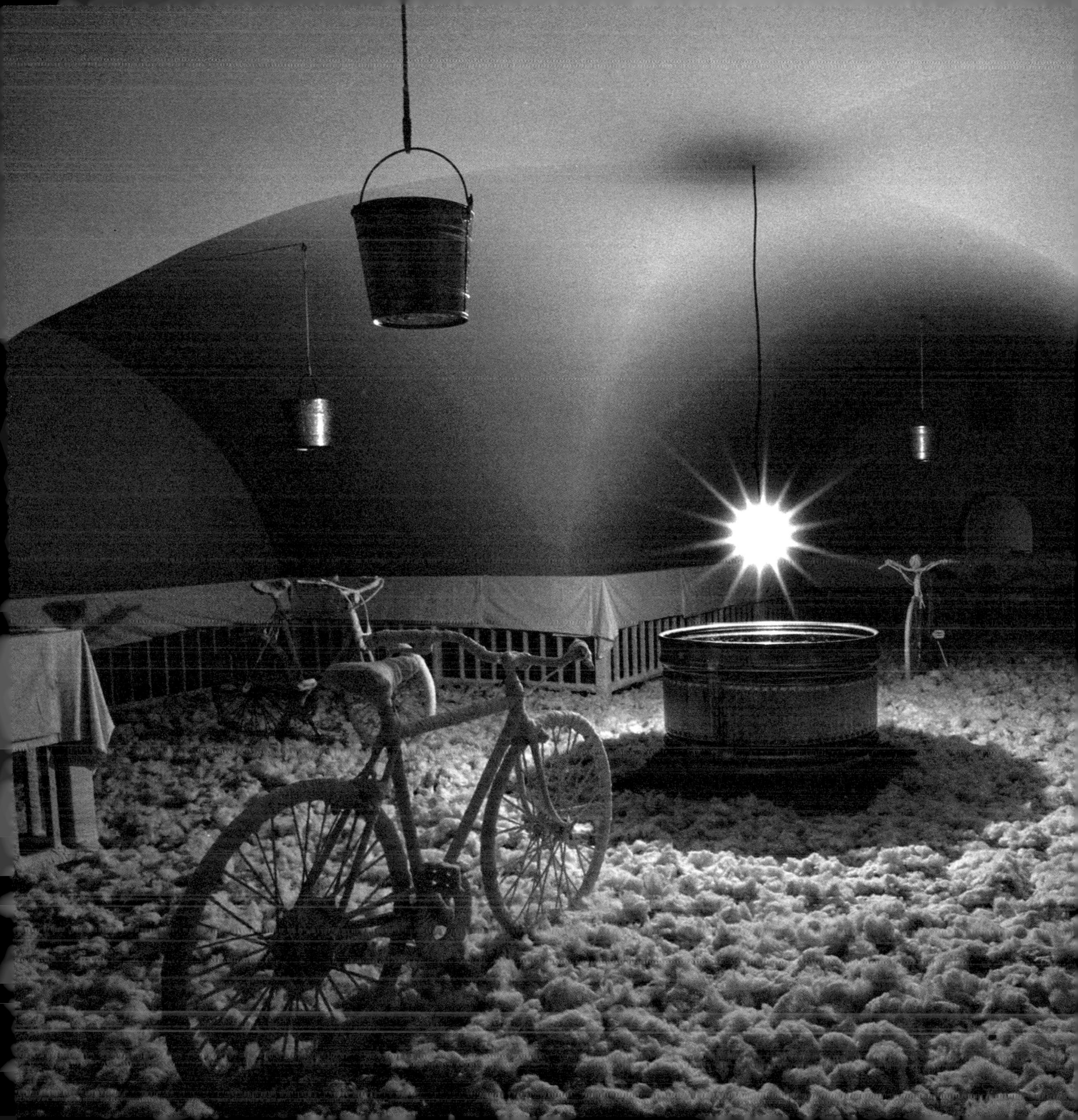

Selected Previous Installations

*Installations are arranged chronologically
by date of completion.*

Self-Portrait
Longwood Gallery, Massachusetts
College of Art, Boston
May 12, 1979

Entering as if attending a theatrical performance,
viewers found a room containing a nine-foot-square
cage made of chicken wire. In the cage were an
armchair, ottoman, and floor lamp. The artist,
dressed in white and seated in the chair, addressed
the audience: "This is a self-portrait. You may ask
me any question you like. If it's too personal, I'll
answer it in Gaelic."

"She Is Not Dead, She Doth Not Sleep"
In "Environmental Works"
Center for Advanced Visual Studies,
Massachusetts Institute of Technology,
Cambridge
May 1979

A mound of soil was packed down into a truncated
pyramid, sixteen feet on a side. Near its top a
wooden fence outlined a triangle, enclosing an
iron grid where the artist could sometimes be found
lying down.

"D'ye Hear Me, Auld Buttergills?"
(fig. 1, photograph by the artist)
In "Environmental Sculpture," a collaborative
exhibition organized by Massachusetts College
of Art alumni and students
Presented at DeCordova and Dana Museum
and Park, Lincoln, Massachusetts
July 27–September 7, 1980

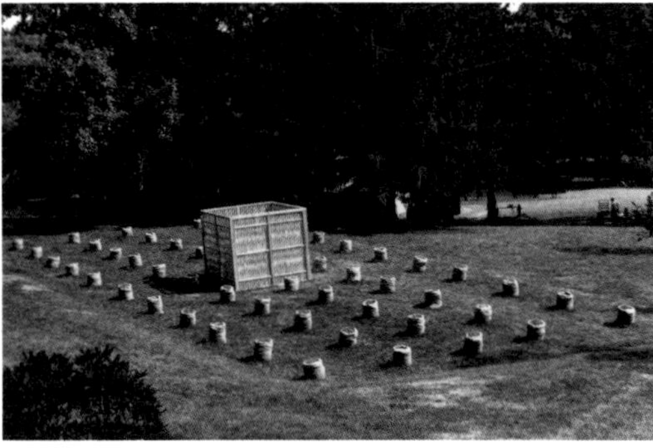

Fig. 1

On an expansive lawn, five long lines of open
burlap sacks formed a rectangle (150 feet wide
by 450 feet long). Centered in the rectangle was
a roofless enclosure, made from interlaced slats;
it was nine feet square and nine feet tall. Visible
through the slats, a truncated pyramid crowned
by an armchair fit snugly inside. The surface of the
pyramid, which was constructed of plywood, was
covered by layers of potatoes (stuck into nails driven
through the wood). As the weeks passed, grass
grew out of the sacks, appearing through the opening as well as through the burlap's weave, and the
potatoes spoiled, attracting swarms of flies as the
process advanced.

"Ah But I Being Young and Foolish"
(fig. 2, photograph by the artist)
In "Michael Timpson: Sculptural Installation"
Helen Shlien Gallery, Boston
October 9–November 1, 1980

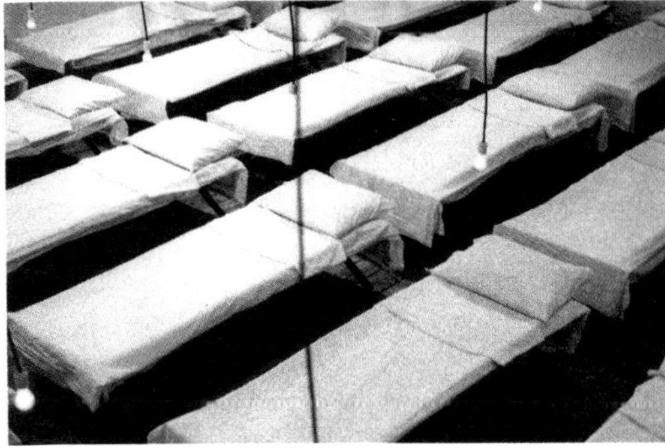

Fig. 2

Neatly made army cots were lined up in rows
on a hardwood floor; a bare white bulb, hanging on a long black cord from the ceiling, was
suspended over the pillow on each bed.

"Now Do You Know"
In "Three Installations"
DeCordova and Dana Museum and Park,
Lincoln, Massachusetts
March 1–April 26, 1981

In a room with the temperature conspicuously low-
ered and lit by a single bare bulb, there were four
rows of metal garbage cans, each with lid propped
against its side and unplugged trouble light suspended from its lip. The rows led up to a wooden
container suggesting a sarcophagus and heaped
with boulders. Outside the balustrade, surround-
ing the rectangle made by cans and "sarcophagus," was a boardwalk for viewers.

"Just Knock Three Times and Whisper Low" (figs. 3 and 4)
Part of "New Works" program
DeCordova and Dana Museum and Park,
Lincoln, Massachusetts
Completed November 1982; dismantled 1989

On the wooded grounds of the park, the artist
built a fifty-foot-square, shingled structure with a
twelve-foot-long entrance hall extending from one
side. The chapel-like building housed four wheelbarrows, each with a spade resting in it. The wheelbarrows were paired and parked on a square of
sunken brick pavement in the center of the space.
This central area was
enclosed by a low, fir
parapet supporting a
square column (also fir)
at each corner and sep-
arating the wheelbar-
rows from the interior's
spruce floor (painted
olive drab). Echoing the
parapet, continuous fir

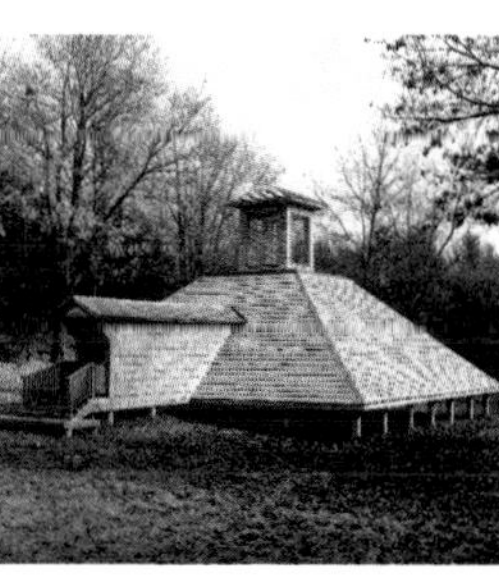

Fig. 3

seating (anchored to the wall) outlined the room's
perimeter, and natural light filtered in through
windows and a vent in the cupola.

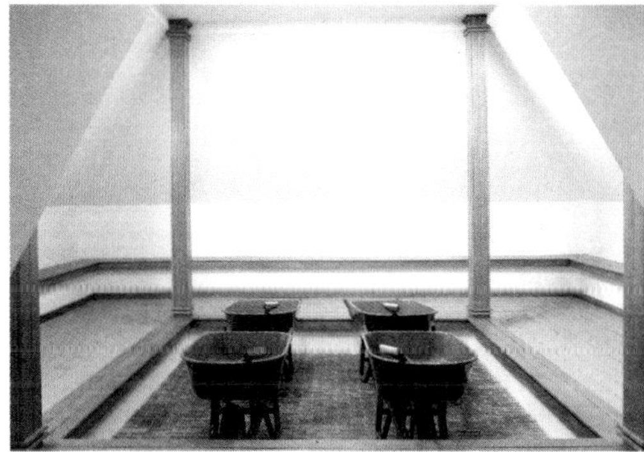

Fig. 4

"What Burns Where the Flame Used to Be" (fig. 5)
In "Michael Timpson—Installation"
Helen Shlien Gallery, Boston
February 2–26, 1983

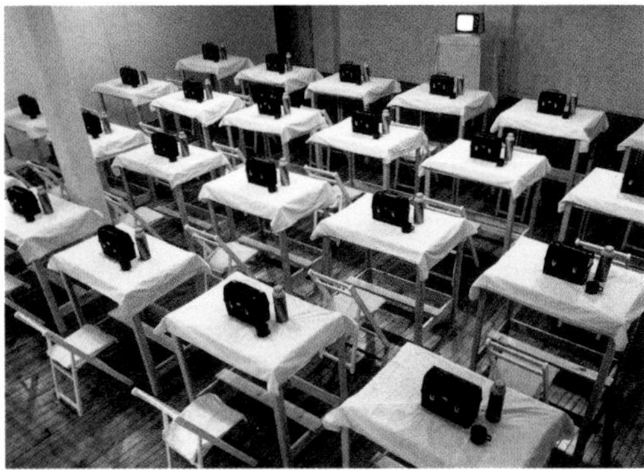

Fig. 5

In a room with minimal track lighting, rows of simple pine tables (built by the artist to be four inches higher than average) faced a television tuned to static. Each table was covered with a white cloth, on which sat a lunch pail, thermos, and cup. Pulled up to each table was a wooden folding chair (commercially made and intentionally chosen for its smaller scale), with a pillowcase folded on its seat.

"Time Up" (for Nana)
Part of "Projects One" series
Danforth Museum of Art,
Framingham, Massachusetts
May 15–July 3, 1983

A dogleg passageway led to a threshold blocked by a large stone, which viewers had to negotiate. Beyond was a small, black room from which emanated the smell of the soil covering its floor. The room contained an ironing board and iron, around which stood shrouded figures (one a person, the others mannequins). Extending from each shroud, an exposed hand suspended a light bulb on a cord over a stone marker.

"Not a Drum Was Heard, Not a Funeral Beat"
In "Brockton Art Museum
Triennial Invitation Exhibition"
Brockton Art Museum (now Fuller Museum of Art),
Brockton, Massachusetts
December 10, 1983–January 29, 1984
Performance December 10, 1983

For the nighttime performance twelve actors took position on the bank of a recently emptied lake. Each kept two flashlights trained on the artist and his collaborator, Dennis Downey, as the pair walked around the lake bed. To the beat of a *bodhrán* (an Irish goatskin drum), the actors repeatedly counted to ten, softly garbling the numbers. A residue of the set remained for the duration of the exhibition: There was a white, rag rope tied around two huge boulders placed 300 yards apart in the drained lake. Parallel to the boulders in a nearby moat were three low, ten-feet-long, stainless steel vats, one piled high with silt from the lake bed, the second with decaying wood, and the third with boulders.

"Be the Boys"
In "Boston Now: Sculpture"
Institute of Contemporary Art, Boston
June 27–August 19, 1984

A stairway led down to a cramped room, divided into seating and stage. Lit by four red bulbs, ten rows of bleachers were divided by a central aisle with fragmented-stone floor. Boulders on folded white pillowcases resting on odorous marsh hay were paired on each section of bleacher. On the stage, behind a window fitted with a wire grid, were two blindfolded, bare-chested, and immobile actors, each seated at a table. The tables held tin buckets into which water dripped steadily. Eight loaves of bread were lined up on the windowsill separating actors from audience.

"I Speak That Am But a Fool" (fig. 6)
Bess Cutler Gallery, New York City
January 3–February 6, 1985

Draped tables, lit by construction lights suspended like hanging lanterns, met to form a rectangle around an open space. There were thirty draped chairs pulled up to the tables and twenty-six places set, each defined by a polished plate holding a head of cabbage. In the inner area, two body casts enclosed in burlap body bags were lying on a red cloth. A pile of three stones was placed at the head of each bag; a coil of hose at the foot. Balanced on each pile of stones was a blue-and-white enameled basin containing pork and beans and a loaf of bread. The floor was covered in straw. An aluminum pail hanging from the ceiling dripped water into a second pail placed on a large stone between the two bagged figures.

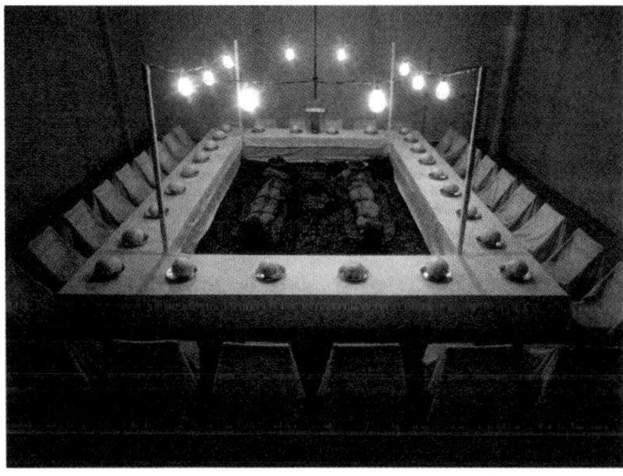

Fig. 6

"Tell Me Why You Hurry So"
In "Michael Timpson: New York"
Helen Shlien Gallery, Boston
May 30–June 27, 1985

Under minimal track lighting, four rows of black, metal, five-gallon buckets hung at head height on ropes wrapped in crimson fabric. Positioned beneath each bucket was an identical one sitting on a white pillow on the hardwood floor; the bottom buckets were draped in crimson cloth. Dead center, there was an armchair covered in white sheeting in which from time to time sat a figure draped, also in white, from head to toe.

"He Will Not Come and Still I Wait"

(fig. 7) Maudslay State Park,
Newburyport, Massachusetts
Sponsored by the Massachusetts State
Department of Environmental Management
October 1986

Stretching across a field bordered by trees were sections of clothesline, strung between pairs of posts, with white bed sheets hanging on the line: four sheets to a section, three sections to a row, eleven rows.

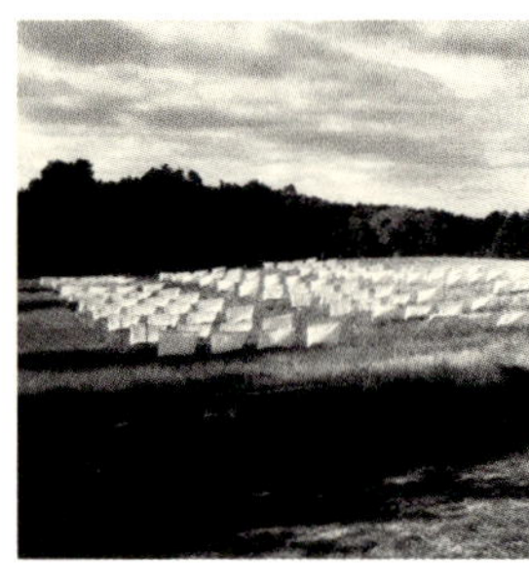

Fig. 7

The posts were wrapped in crimson fabric, and each was topped with a head of cabbage on a polished aluminum plate.

"Be the Holy"

Accompanied by artist's statement,
"My Father's Tools Sit Silently"
(see bibliography under Timpson)
In "Installations 3"
Philadelphia Art Alliance
January 12–March 14, 1987

Draped chairs were provided where viewers could remove their shoes before entering a windowless room, the walls, ceiling, and floor of which had been covered with white fabric. In the middle of the room, a continuous prie-dieu enclosed a rectangular space. At regular intervals folio-size books lay open, the text of each almost completely obscured by a black cloth extending lengthwise over its pages. A pillow cushioning the kneeler marked the placement of each book. In the central space were six porcelain toilets, two rows of three each, with their tanks draped in red cloth. On top of each tank was an open book (also folio-size) resting on a pillow. Above each book hung a round fluorescent fixture. Potatoes filled the floor space around the toilets.

A Peculiar Hunger

Collaboration with performance artist
Dennis Downey
In "Boston Now: Projects"
Institute of Contemporary Art, Boston
June 26–August 30, 1987

To enter, a viewer had to duck behind a grille that resembled an old-fashioned radiator and squeeze through a small door. Once inside, the compressed space forced him to sit. (Pillows were provided.) Downey, dressed in white and carrying a staff, occupied a shallow stage where he delivered extemporaneous monologues. On an abbreviated runway projecting from the stage, there was a wooden pallet under a bare bulb where Downey sometimes reclined. Around the runway were rows of open burlap sacks filled with soil. Wrapped columns held up a nonfunctional balcony above which 500 loaves of Wonder Bread lined the ceiling. A yeasty smell became pervasive.

"Have You Gone with the Snows of Last Winter?"
In conjunction with the Massachusetts
Artists Foundation Fellowship
Installed at the Massachusetts State
Transportation Building, in the concourse
of CityPlace, Boston
March 1988

Arranged in a ring on the concourse's brick pavement were six porcelain toilets, each facing out.
Resting on a pillow on top of each tank was a thick,
folio-size book (the *Congressional Record*), lying
open and draped lengthwise with a strip of black
cloth. Scattered across the circle outlined by the toilets were bags made from squares of white fabric
filled with sand and tied up with black cloth bands.

"Bearing the Rabbit" (fig. 8)
In "New England Now:
Contemporary Art from Six States"
Bowdoin College Museum of Art,
Brunswick, Maine
July 1–September 4, 1988
Note: Only the preparatory drawings for
Bearing the Rabbit" were shown at the five
other sites to which "New England Now"
traveled between 1987and 1989.

Stepping over a large Maine boulder, viewers
walked through a narrow, curtained tunnel into an
oval room. A boardwalk and a balustrade wrapped
in bed sheets outlined the room's perimeter. At
regular intervals along the balustrade were metal
washbasins, filled with water, each accompanied
by a folded white towel and a bar of soap. On the
floor, marking the placement of each basin, a
local granite boulder jutted through the board-

walk. Just inside the balustrade, echoing its oval
shape, were rows of canned pork and beans; these
surrounded a rectangle made by four long lines of
feed sacks. The necks of the sacks were rolled
down, revealing their contents—sterilized topsoil,
moistened by periodic spraying to ensure a pun-
gent aroma. The sacks rested on pallets (converted
garden trellises) sprinkled with wood shavings.
Seated in the soil in the top of each sack was a
ticking, brass alarm clock. The gallery's four niches
were lined with curtains; each, lit by a red bulb,
enshrined an open, folio-size book inclined on a
large granite rock used as a bookrest. Overhead,

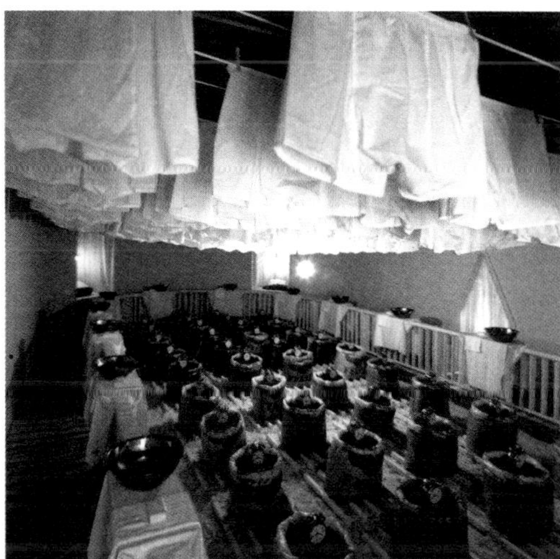

Fig. 8

rows of clothesline ran from one end of the room
to the other; hanging from them were hundreds of
pairs of boxer shorts swaying slightly in the air
movement generated by the room's cooling system.

"Up in the Bogs"
Stux Gallery, New York City
March 8–April 1, 1989

Rows of red fire buckets, handles raised, were evenly spaced across the gallery's hardwood floor under minimal track lighting. Folded over each bucket was a pair of white boxer shorts. In alternate rows, every other bucket was covered with a white-cased pillow on which was placed a wrapped board and two black fabric scrolls. The board supported a standing wrapped shovel, scoop pointed down. Strapped to the shovel's handle was another wrapped board supporting an open, folio-size book. A long, black cloth band was draped widthwise across the pages; on top sat a two-belled, brass alarm clock which rang regularly at twelve o'clock.

"It's a Far Cry" (fig. 9)
Accompanied by artist's statement
(published in exhibition catalogue; see
bibliography under *Project: Installation*)
In "Project: Installation"
The Aldrich Museum of Contemporary Art,
Ridgefield, Connecticut
October 29, 1989–February 25, 1990

A narrow corridor led through a keyhole-shaped opening into a low-ceilinged room. The room's center was defined by a rectangle of plywood flooring covered with a two-inch-deep layer of loose rice, through which protruded hundreds of evenly spaced nails. Placed on the plywood was a cast-iron and brass bed, bedstead wrapped with white cloth and mattress dressed in white bed linens. Attached to the wall behind the headboard were white-cased pillows, three rows of three each, each holding an open folio-size book. Symmetrically arranged around the bed and resting on the nail points were metal washbasins containing water. Upended, wrapped shovels outlined this raised

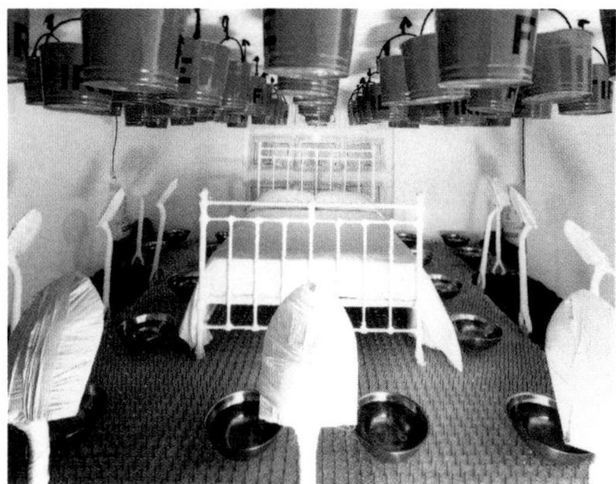

Fig. 9

rectangular area. Between the "balustrade" of shovels and the room's walls was a walkway of coal. Corner niches each contained a bag of rice on a pile of stones, illuminated by a suspended red bulb. Twenty-four red fire buckets, each holding a ticking alarm clock, hung from the ceiling.

"The Mickey Ruz" (fig. 10)
White Columns, New York City
May 29–June 30, 1991

Signage asked viewers to remove their shoes and alerted them to capacity restrictions—the enclosed space could accommodate only two at a time. Faced with a choice of entrances, viewers had to turn either left or right on a narrow passageway, the walkway of which was covered twelve inches deep with turkey feathers (fluffed daily). The interior space had a peaked ceiling, and its floor was lined with half a foot of coal supporting a symmetrical arrangement of four pillows. On each pillow was a metal grid holding a hot plate and a long-handled, stainless steel saucepan (all four handles in alignment). In the pan a white egg cooked in boiling water, effectively raising the humidity level in the room. (Both the egg and the water were replaced regularly.) At the front of the cramped space was a low table, its top and legs wrapped in white fabric. A round loaf of bread, with an impressed *X* baked in its crust, sat on the table, over which a black flashlight (the single source of light) was suspended. Also hanging from the ceiling were four push brooms, their broomsticks forming a line of verticals down the center of the room and positioned so that the broom heads with their rigid bristles confronted viewers at eye level.

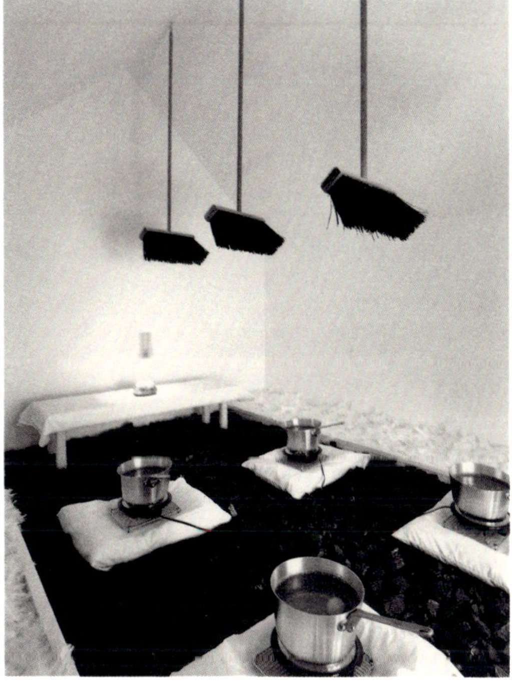

Fig. 10

Biography

Michael Timpson was born on February 15, 1951, in Athy, a farming community forty miles southwest of Dublin, in County Kildare, Ireland. Memories of his childhood there lend piquancy and color to his work. In particular, his feisty paternal grandmother, who was, Timpson says, "in touch with another world," sparked his imagination with her beguiling tales of fairies and banshees as well as an ongoing narrative describing her own life. There were other reverberating influences. Timpson was receptive to not only the spoken but also the written word. The native son's absorption in his country's haunting literary legacy began at an early age; learning much verse by heart has left him with an easy—and enviable—familiarity with the great Irish and English poets. Timpson's approach to learning in general was governed by the discipline of hard work and strict obedience instilled in him at the Christian Brothers secondary school in Athy. While he was a student (and for a year after he graduated), Timpson worked with his father, a foreman in a small commercial foundry. About this apprenticeship with a man he revered, he has said, "I learned a trade there and the meaning of craft." He also acquired firsthand knowledge of his father's workday—and life's work—a legacy with lasting import.

Ever since he was a child, Timpson had spent time drawing, an artistic inclination that was reinforced by contact with a sculptor-friend of his oldest brother's. A profession that combined the use of head and hands appealed to Timpson. However, rather than attending the National College of Art and Design in Dublin, in deference to parental concern about job security he went instead to University College there. Entering in the fall of 1972, he took courses in the history of European painting and pre-Celtic archaeology. While he enjoyed the art history, the teaching method distanced him too much from the art itself. Of greater benefit was the course-required travel to Italy, providing the direct experience lacking in the lecture hall. Another responsive chord was struck by the introduction to archaeology. The subject came naturally to Timpson, for he had grown up in the presence of the ancient burial mounds around Athy. Formal study of the megalithic builders' passage graves supplied the artist with ideas that continue to infiltrate his work. It was also at University College that he encountered the American sculptor Robert Cronin, who interested him in Massachusetts College of Art in Boston.

A sustained desire to extricate himself from a life he found restrictive led Timpson to emigrate. Having decided to study art in the United States, he arrived in this country in the summer of 1973. After a brief interlude on a ranch near Arcadia, Florida, where he played out a boyhood fantasy of being a cowboy, Timpson moved to the Boston area. His first year there he had a daytime job in a Somerville laundry and went to night school, studying welding with George Greenamyer who was on the faculty of Massachusetts College of Art and proved to be a sympathetic teacher. (Timpson had the reassuring feeling that Greenamyer understood what he was after, early on perceiving that his student's work had a deep involvement with theater.)

In 1975, Timpson gained admission to Massachusetts College of Art, where he concentrated on writing and sculpture, weighing the verbal against the visual, trying to settle on the right form of expression for himself. A contemporary sculpture course taught by Johanna Gill covered the work of Joseph Beuys, Richard Serra, Edward Kienholz, and Robert Smithson, among others. The course opened up a new world for Timpson, exposing him to artists whose work energized him (and affects him still). Always an outlet for him, writing from this point on yielded to art. By his senior year Timpson had departed from what he describes as the "Anthony Caro–type sculpture" he had been doing; he began experimenting with installations.

After graduating in 1979 with a B.F.A., Timpson met Helen Shlien, a Boston gallery owner supportive of installation art. A critical contact for him, she gave Timpson his first one-man exhibition, in 1980. At that time opportunities to show such work in Boston were rare, and there was much disappointment when she closed her gallery in 1985 (with a Timpson installation as the final show). Timpson acknowledges the significant contribution Shlien has made to his development as an artist.

In the early 1980s the artist began receiving commissions from various organizations in Massachusetts, while showing regularly at the Shlien gallery. In 1981 he was included in his first museum-organized show, at the DeCordova and Dana Museum and Park in Lincoln, Massachusetts (a museum that would become a frequent host to his installations). Timpson was earning increasing recognition—and notoriety—for his work. In some cases, concerned officials required adjustments or even re-moval, to the compliant—if somewhat baffled—artist's mild amusement.

During his final year in college, Timpson had taken courses at the Center for Advanced Visual Studies at Massachusetts Institute of Technology in Cambridge; and in 1984 he returned there, enrolling in Otto Piene's environmental art program in order to learn the technology behind large-scale outdoor sculpture. In 1985 he had his first solo show in New York City, at the Bess Cutler Gallery. Throughout the 1980s his installations were in important group exhibitions in the Northeast, and his drawings were also being shown. Timpson has consistently been involved in diverse activities outside the traditional museum setting. He has, for example, in collaboration with performance artist Ellen Rothenberg, designed a temporary installation for a Boston subway station during its renovation (part of the city's "Arts on the Line" program). There have been other collaborations; one was with the sound artist John Ewart. The two were commissioned by Mobius to do a piece for the 1987 Sound Art Festival in Boston. That same year Timpson won a prestigious $9,500 Massachusetts Artists Foundation Fellowship.

Timpson moved to New York City in 1987, where he supports himself, as he did in Boston, by working as a carpenter. (In Massachusetts he operated a home-building business, and in New York he has his own carpentry-contracting business.) In the city, Timpson has shown at Stux Gallery and at the alternative space White Columns, where he will participate in an autumn 1991 "Update" exhibition. The Rotunda Gallery in the artist's home borough of Brooklyn has commissioned an installation for January 1992, and future projects are scheduled for Poland and Turkey. In Warsaw, for a show being organized by Kim Levin, Timpson and five other American artists will create site-specific installations using indigenous materials. He will also be part of an Istanbul exhibition which the painter Sukran Aziz is planning. The show will bring together Turkish and American works of art, with improvisational percussive collaboration provided by the jazz drummer Billy Higgins.

Since 1973, the artist has been married to Maryanne Shannon, an American he met when both were students at University College. After working as an independent filmmaker and producer, Shannon is now a doctoral student in film history at New York University. The couple's son, Oengus, was born in Ireland and is currently a freshman at the University of Iowa in Iowa City.

Selected Bibliography

Beem, Edgar Allen. *"Bearing the Rabbit." Maine Times,* 8 July 1988, 25.

Bonetti, David. "Michael Timpson." *Art New England* (March 1983): 7.

Brenson, Michael. "Michael Timpson." *New York Times,* 1 February 1985, C24.

Giuliano, Charles, and Eugene Narrett. "The ICA: Two Views."
Art New England (September 1987): 28–29.

Hoey, Dennis. "Artist Gives Birth to a 'Rabbit' at Bowdoin."
Portland Press Herald, 2 July 1988, 11–12.

Koplos, Janet. "Art 'Installations' on Display at the Aldrich Museum."
(Stamford, Conn.) *Advocate and Greenwich Time,* 19 November 1989, D1.

Levin, Kim. "Art: Altar Egos." *Village Voice,* 5 February 1985, 86.

———. "Choices: Michael Timpson." *Village Voice,* 28 March 1989, 44.

———. "Choices: Fred Tomaselli/Michael Timpson." *Village Voice,* 2 July 1991, 102.

McFadden, Sarah. "Report from Boston." *Art in America* (May 1983): 33–43.

Monegain, Bernie. "'Different' Art Show Comes to the College."
(Brunswick, Maine) *Times Record,* 28 June 1988, 1, 20.

Montagu, Kyra. "Art at Maudslay." *Art New England*
(December 1986–January 1987): 15.

New England Now: Contemporary Art from Six States. Brunswick, Maine:
Bowdoin College Museum of Art, 1987.

Project: Installation. Ridgefield, Connecticut: Aldrich Museum of Contemporary Art, 1989.

Sozanski, Edward J. "Through Galleries' Windows, Tiny Reflections of Ourselves."
Philadelphia Inquirer, 26 February 1987, 5-C.

Stapen, Nancy. "The Consumer Product and Sculpture: Michael Timpson."
Art New England (May 1985): 5.

————. "ICA/MFA: The Follies Bizarre." *Art New England*
(July–August 1984): 4–5, 21.

Tarlow, Lois. "Profile: Michael Timpson." *Art New England*
(March 1987):14–15, 19.

Taylor, Robert. "The DeCordova Presents a Beguiling Blend."
Boston Globe, 29 March 1981, A26.

Temin, Christine. "Bowled Over." *Boston Globe,* 4 March 1988; 1, 22.

————. "Timpson Installation Filled with Intrigue."
Boston Globe, 13 June 1985, 89.

————. "The Wonder of Art and Words."
Boston Globe, 16 July 1987, 13.

Timpson, Michael. "Special Places: 'My Father's Tools Sit Silently.'"
Art New England (Summer 1986): 7.

————. *"Time Up"* (for Nana) [illus. only].
Art New England (June 1983): 13.

Zimmer, William. "The Aldrich Fills Its Rooms with Expansive Sculptures."
New York Times (Conn. ed.), 12 November 1989, 36.